RAILWAY RAMBLES

ON THE

CHESHIRE LINES

C. T. GOODE

1987

ISBN 1 870313 01 1

72 Woodland Drive, Anlaby. Hull. HU10 7HX

RAILWAY RAMBLES
ON THE
CHESHIRE LINES

The Cheshire Lines Committee was an unusual concern, well connected and strategically linked on all sides, active and yet without a single engine of its own, apart from four steam railcars. Its letters could be found blazoned on wagons, coaches and brake vans, and many of these 'escaped' during wartime, so that the Author was puzzled when a youngster to see 'C L' on an otherwise perfectly normal brake van which had got itself into the lesser known sidings round Doncaster, no doubt lingering there until someone in authority caught on and sent it packing. 'C L' was certainly easier to apply to wagon sides than the original title which would have been: 'the GN and MS & L Joint Committee' which was formed in 1860. 'Cheshire Lines' was in fact peculiar in itself, as much of the committee's activity lay in Lancashire.

In 1860 powers were sought for two lines, the Stockport & Woodley Railway of a good two miles in length which was opened on 12th January, 1863 and connected with the line from Woodley to Manchester. The second line was the Cheshire Midland, twelve miles long and an extension of the Manchester, South Jc. and Altrincham line, opened to Knutsford on 12th May, 1862 and to Northwich on 1st January, 1863. Other pieces of the jigsaw were the Stockport, Timperley and Altrincham, nine miles in length, opened in February 1866 and a further section at Woodley, opened to Godley in 1866.

From Northwich the West Cheshire Railway of 1861 took trains out to Helsby and to a junction with the Birkenhead Joint line. The Winsford and Winnington branches came into being in 1869 and 1870 respectively.

In 1861 the GN and MS & L companies obtained joint powers to construct a line from Garston to Liverpool Brunswick Dock, which was opened on 1st June, 1864, and running powers were granted over the London and North Western between Broadheath and Garston to enable a liaison between the Liverpool and Stockport sections to develop. In 1864 powers were obtained to build a short section of line from Brunswick to a site for a Liverpool Central station.

In July, 1866 two momentous events occurred, the first being the adoption of the Midland Railway as a third member of the Committee; the second being the passing of the Act to construct 36 miles of railway from Garston to Cornbrook Jc., Manchester, the new main line of the CLC, as well as the southern cross-route from Glazebrook to Timperley. The last major line opened was that between Mouldsworth and Chester Northgate, opened in 1874 under the terms of the Cheshire & West Cheshire Junction Railways Act.

Together with the Southport & Cheshire Lines Extension Railway which was worked by agreement, all the above made up the CLC and the Act of August 1867 summarised the whole, neatly apportioning equal shares to the three companies involved and permitting three directors from each to serve on the committee of nine. Messrs. Watkin, Fenton and Turner were the first MS & L members of the committee, possibly the most active committee of the group as the motive power and station buildings owed much to its influence. The total mileage was 143½ and, initially, the head offices were in Alexandra Buildings, James St. Liverpool, where passengers could book, being conveyed by horse drawn omnibus to Brunswick station. The vehicles' wheels conveniently dropped into the dock railway lines which were of the tram type in several of the streets, thus providing an unwitting early tram ride. In 1874 the line had reached Ranelagh Street and the site of Hengler's Circus where the new station was constructed, along with new offices to match. At Grouping in 1923 the LNER had six directors and the LMS three on the Board.

It was a brave act to launch a new hybrid railway in an area already efficiently catered for by two rivals, the Lancashire & Yorkshire and North Western companies. Yet the CLC had much to offer and put up impressive runs with its rivals between Liverpool and Manchester, as witness extracts from the 1942 timetable:

Manchester Central dep:	9.30 a.m.	Liverpool Central arr:	10.23. Two stops.
Manchester Exchange dep:	8.58 a.m.	Liverpool Lime St. arr.:	9.52. Three stops.
Manchester Vic. dep:	9.35 a.m.	Liverpool Exchange arr:	10.29. Non-stop.

The first was CLC and took 53 minutes the fastest of the three; the second was ex LNWR with the easiest route and three stops, while the L & Y was non-stop. Both these took 54 minutes.

Traffic could pass on to and leave the CLC at thirteen junctions, among the most important being Cornbrook, Glazebrook for Wigan and St. Helens, Helsby for Birkenhead and with Chester for North Wales stations. The ICI and Salt Union Company at Northwich and Winsford were almost completely reliant on the CLC for shipments by rail. The Manchester Ship Canal Company was opened on 1st January, 1894 and its cutting caused the building of vast embankments with the spoil with viaducts to heights of 43 feet to cross it. The Canal Co. had its own rail system which worked closely with the CLC serving the vast industrial estates such as Trafford Park.

The Cheshire Lines system has not hitherto attracted such attention from railway historians and writers of books, probably because it never had a history of motive power development of its own. To the ordinary enthusiast the CLC was like being on the Great Central on the wrong side of the country, with old familiar and often expiring friends at the head of the trains, such as the 'Directors' and smaller D9s which, alas, were not cleaned and maintained as well as they had been at sheds such as Mexborough even during the war period. The high point of the Author's acquaintance with the Cheshire Lines was a well remembered footplate trip from Manchester Central out to Glazebrook on 'Sir Edward Fraser' and a chance to work the controls, all highly illegal of course, but his enthusiastic looks from down on the platform must have swayed the crew. On returning to Central there then followed the run to Trafford Park shed, a dreadful, roofless place to work in during its last years and a living graveyard for the GC element which was scattered about the place in various stages of decay. The Midland brigade seemed to fare somewhat better.

The most unique feature about the CLC was its signals with curious arms which went up when they ought to have descended and with posts of oblong section. The signal boxes were unique in design, too, with large nameboards across their fronts. I make no apology, therefore, for including a lot of Mr. Johnson's excellent cabin photographs and hope the reader will enjoy the little collection which should be taken in conjunction with the history of the Company in the Oakwood Press series.

C. Tony Goode BA.
Anlaby, Hull. 1987

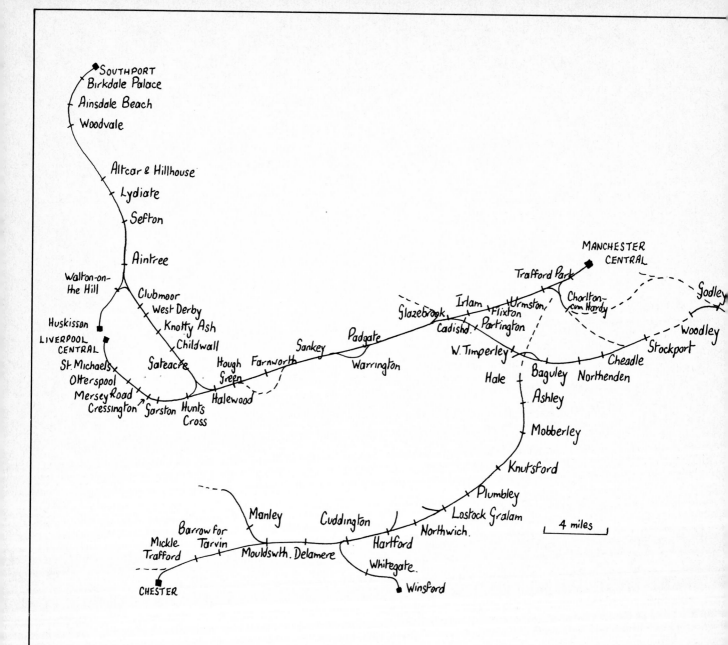

The CLC System

1. A view of the interior of Northwich signal box with a signal close at hand outside.

2. Sandbach Junction cabin, Northwich, giving the destination of the branch which left at this point.

2

3. Knutsford West signal box, a vertically boarded timber affair.

4. Signal bracket at
Glazebrook East Junction with
upper quadrant arms of a
curious pattern, introduced in
the 1930s and made at the
Company's works at Battersby
Lane, Warrington.

5. At Macket's Lane, Hunt's
Cross, the Gateacre line signal
shows 'clear'.

6. Further examples at
Halewood North Junction.

7. Mouldsworth Junction.

7

8. A taller signal cabin at Hartford Junction, governing the spur to the LNWR main line.

9. Signal at Aintree, looking
suspiciously as if the upper
arm goes up and the lower
descends!

10. Delamere signal box.

10

11. A more orthodox design at Plumley West, on the Northwich line.

12. Three views of Garston station, an important place on the local service out of Liverpool Central, showing the distinctive looking office at road level.

13

2

13. The platform structure after closure in the 1960s.

16

14

1

14. – and a general view looking west at about the same time.

15. Nearer in to Liverpool was Mersey Road & Aigburth station with its jolly striped flounces.

16. The station was not so happy in this pre-renovation view in 1978.

17. Otterspool, next to Mersey Road, was similar and seems to have been overlooked in the later Merseyrail thinking. The building was latterly still there and resembled its neighbour. The station closed in March, 1951.

18. Cressington &
Grassendale was given the full
renovation treatment, as
befitted its sonorous name.

18

19. At Hunt's Cross trains
could turn north for the
Southport Extension line via
Gateacre, seen here in 1955.

20. Another view, this time of the exterior with nameboard.

21. Before Aintree was reached, a few trains ran west to Walton-on-the-Hill and back, on the Huskisson Dock line. The station is seen here in this rare view of 1950.

22. Further north towards Southport was Sefton & Maghull.

22

23. Unprepossessing Woodvale.

4

24. Birkdale Palace, an island affair on the sands.

25

25. Southport Lord Street, an imposing terminus at the end of a 3½ mile run along the sand dunes. This closed in 1952 and became a bus station.

26. Northwich was a substantial station on the line out to Chester, which was extended from Mouldsworth.

26

27. Hartford & Greenbank station lay further out towards Chester and shared traffic with that on the LNWR main line nearby.

28

29

28. In 1911 a day trip to New Brighton is seen leaving Mickle Trafford station, just outside Chester. The station was a modest affair which closed on 12th February, 1951.

29. The station at Mouldsworth, showing in the background the tall junction signals for the Helsby branch.

30. Inside Chester Northgate station, showing roofwork and CLC rolling stock.

30

31. The approach to Chester Northgate.

32. At Cuddington a branch wound its way southwards, serving first Whitegate

2

33

33. and running to the terminus at Winsford & Over which closed to passengers in 1931 and totally in 1968. The LNWR had a short branch to Over & Wharton nearby.

34. Once the Midland Railway
had joined the Cheshire Lines
Committee, then the main
route between Liverpool and
Manchester was developed,
with fine stations at each end.
Here is Liverpool Central
station (and Lewis's
emporium) on a prime site.

34

35. With a proud driver, GC
Class 11a No. 5877 (LNER
D6) in green livery prepares to
leave Liverpool Central.

36

36. The fine roof of Manchester Central station, built by John Fowler with a span of 210ft., 30ft. less than St. Pancras and blazoning the railways on offer. The bus is marked 'forces only'.

37

37. LMR. 2.6.4 tank No. 42583 rests under the vault of Manchester Central.

38. Out in the sunshine, a
Class D9 4.4.0 No. 6013
relaxes with a friendly J11 No.
4374.

38

39

39. An ex GER 'Claud' No.
62535 makes a getaway from
Manchester Central in April
1951. These 'foreign'
locomotives displaced the GC
motive power and were not
popular.

40

40. One of the older ex GC
4.4.0s enters Sale, near
Altrincham in April 1947.

41

41. A neat array of station
lamps at Flixton, out on the
main line.

42. Detail of awning and bracket scrolls at Flixton.

42

4

43. A well-filled station platform at Urmston.

44. An up-to-date view of Flixton.

45

45. On a more massive scale was Padgate station.

46. Warrington Central, the new image with a new booking office on the Up side.

46

4.

47. Renumbered D9 No. 2325 passes Glazebrook on a Manchester express.

48. An unidentified Class D10 performs the same task at Glazebrook in 1951.

49. Midland Compound No. 41151 passes Garston in August 1954. The line in the left background leads to the LNWR.

50. Cheadle station on the Stockport Tiviot Dale to Glazebrook line.

50

5

51. Compound 41195 leaves Manchester Central in April 1951.

52. 'Britannia' No.70014 'Iron Duke' at Manchester Central.

53

53. Traffic activity at Warrington Central in June 1951.

54. The day begins at Hough Green.

54

5

55. A GC 'Single' No.960 hurries an express through Halewood.

56. Class D11 No. 62666 'Zeebrugge' and D10 No. 62657 'Sir Berkeley Sheffield' at Trafford Park.

57

57. The same team, this time with one of the engine crews.

38

58. A mixed bag at Liverpool Brunswick shed.

58

59. Mainly Midland inside Liverpool Brunswick shed.

60. A 2.6.4. tank No. 42349 at Brunswick shed.

61

61. 'Sir Edward Fraser' and crew at Glazebrook.

62. CLC staff and No. 5859 in wartime.

62

63. D11 No. 62661 'Gerard Powys Dewhurst' and D10 No. 62657 'Prince George' inside Trafford Park shed.

64. A brace of J10s and
'Zeebrugge' outside Trafford
Park shed.

65

65. The approach to Liverpool
Brunswick shed with the main
lines serving Liverpool Central
station.

42

66

6

66. Brunswick shed 'beyond the wall'.

67. Warrington station staff.

68. Class 9F 2.10.0 No. 92218 at Northwich 29.2.1968.

69. The south end from Northwich station.

70. Class 8F No. 48036 leaves
Northwich on an ICI hopper
train. 1.3.1968.

71. No. 42584 enters Mersey Road station in August 1957.

71

72. Class 9F No. 92218 in Northwich station. 29.2.1968.

73. 74. The great CLC goods warehouse at Warrington Central.

74

75. The approach to Glazebrook from Stockport at Cadishead over the Manchester Ship Canal.

75

76. CLC coach No. M4 at Manchester Central, April 1951.

77. CLC articulated set Nos. 705/6 at Manchester Central.

78

78. CLC non-corridor third No.269 at Wentworth Jc. April 1947.

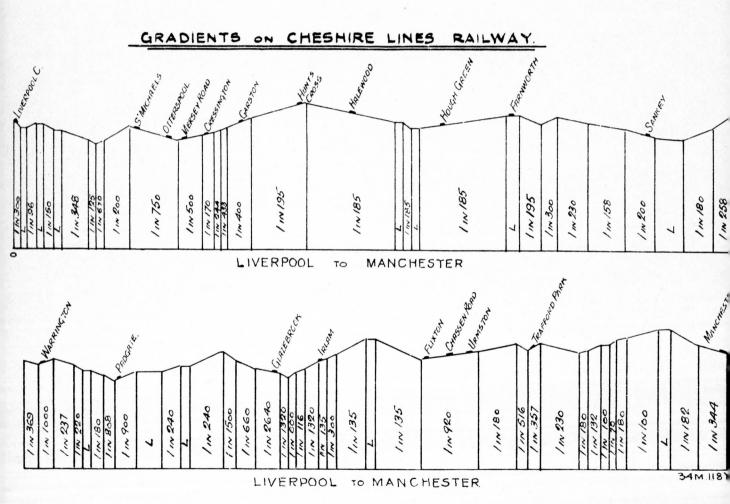

GRADIENTS ON CHESHIRE LINES RAILWAY.

LIVERPOOL TO MANCHESTER

LIVERPOOL TO MANCHESTER

34M.118Y

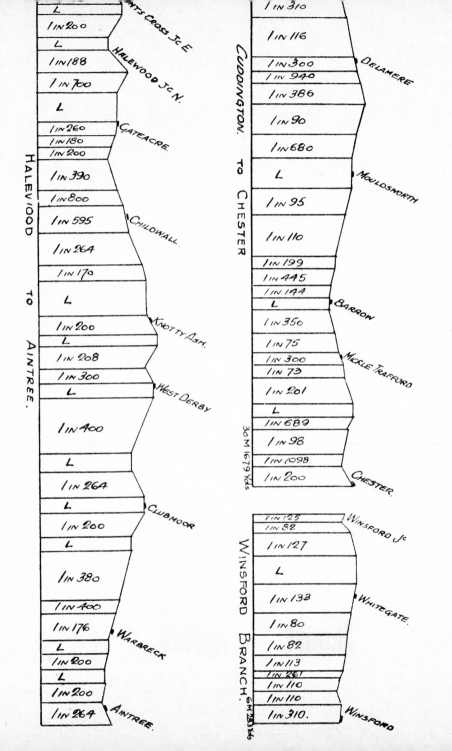

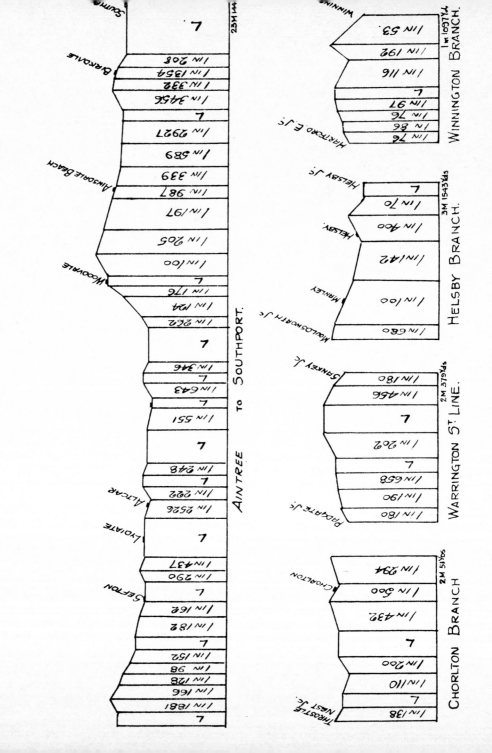

52

THE LIVERPOOL CENTRAL RAILWAY STATION.

MR. JOHN FOWLER, ENGINEER.

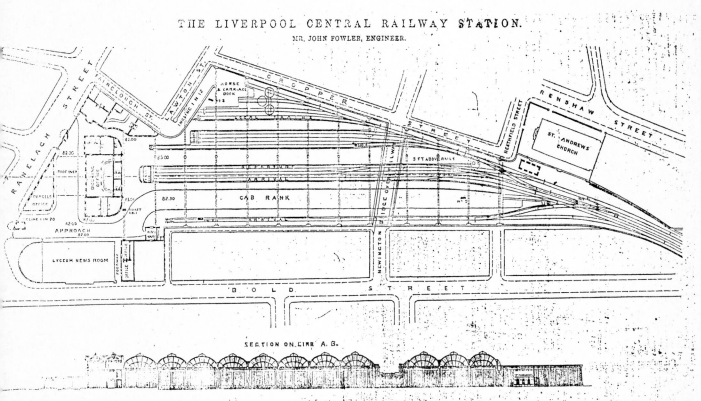

SECTION ON LINE A. B.

THE central railway station at Liverpool about to be constructed occupies a triangular space of ground between Bold and Cropper-streets, and faces on the north upon Ranelagh-street. The general arrangement is shown upon the small accompanying plan, where all the lines of rails, sidings, and platform accommodation are drawn. It will be seen that the Ranelagh-street frontage is not parallel to the station building, but follows the line of the thoroughfare, hence it appears that a somewhat awkward arrangement of the offices was unavoidable. On the east side are placed the refreshment rooms giving upon Fairclough-street, and occupying a considerable space, which is filled with the waiting room and necessary offices at the back, a

distant from it; the intermediate space being covered in by a roof forming a shelter in front of the station. The principals of the roof are light iron structures, with an arched upper member of T-iron, and a straight lower member of the same section, with bar and L-iron bracings. Seven of these principals are employed in the roof, which is glazed with ⅛ in. fluted plate glass. The station building, which stands in the middle of the frontage as shown in the plan, covers an area of about 140 ft. by 65 ft., and is divided on the ground floor into waiting-rooms and booking office. This latter is placed in the middle of the building, and occupies a clear space 75 ft. by 84 ft., 17 ft. 3 in. being taken up for the ticket-offices, and right and left of which

are at the back. As will be seen from the general elevation upon the two-page engraving, the station building has two storeys above the ground floor, the central part of the first one, being occupied with the booking-office, the roof of which is on a level with the second storey of the building. A balcony 6 ft. wide, supported upon ornamental cast-iron brackets, and protected by an ornamental railing, runs round three sides of the booking-office at this level, giving access to the various rooms upon the first floor, which is occupied with the offices and board-room of the company. The second floor is also set aside for official purposes. The walls of the station to the back of the building enclose an

space of one being taken up with a bridge towards the south end, conveying Newington-street over the railway. It is shown on the plan that a row of columns runs down the main platform to carry the girders from which the roof principals spring. The chief details of the roof are given on the two-page engraving. The columns supporting the girders are 35 ft. in height from the platform to the upper side of the cap, with octagonal plinths 2 ft. 1 in. across, reduced to 1 ft. 11 in. at the necking beneath the capital. The base and 18 in. at the base plate upon which each column stands is also octagonal, 4 ft. across from side to side, and 2 in.

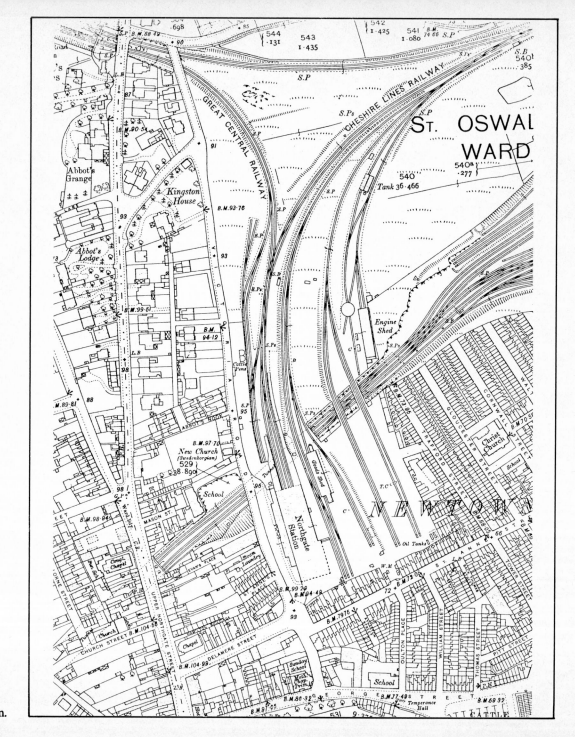

Chester
CLC Station.

CHESHIRE LINES RAILWAY.

DURING THE MONTHS OF

June, July, August and September,

VISITORS to

LLANDUDNO

OR

MENAI BRIDGE

From Manchester, Stockport, Warrington and other Lancashire and Cheshire Towns, cannot do better than travel by the popular, convenient route via

Liverpool (Central)

AND THE

Liverpool and North Wales S.S. Co.'s Steamers.

Convenient service of Express Trains to and from Liverpool (Central) in connection with these Steamers.

Electric Tram Cars pass Liverpool Central Station to and from the Landing Stage every minute.

STOCKPORT TIVIOT DALE STATION—PASSENGER.
STOCKPORT WELLINGTON ROAD—GOODS.

Telephone Numbers ... ... **Passenger Department—5291.**
Goods Department—2753.

STOCKPORT TIVIOT DALE PASSENGER STATION is provided with every facility for dealing with passengers, parcels, horses, live stock, carriages, and miscellaneous traffic.

There is a good service of trains to and from Manchester, and passengers can also be booked to the North-East Coast, East Coast, Midlands, and West and South of England.

Excursion tickets are issued to Southport, Chester, Liverpool and New Brighton, also to the North Wales Coast, Isle of Man, and Ireland via Liverpool and direct steamer, particulars of which may be obtained at the station and town offices.

Parcels for conveyance by the Cheshire Lines Railway for all parts by express trains may be handed in at Tiviot Dale Station.

Free Collection and Delivery.—Upon application to the Station Master at Tiviot Dale Station, vans will call whenever required for the collection of parcels, etc., traffic at any of the warehouses, stores, shops, or other places of business within the usual delivery boundary without extra charge.

Luggage in Advance for all parts of Great Britain served by the Cheshire Lines Railway and its connections is collected similarly upon application.

Wellington Road Goods Station is situated in Wellington Road, and is provided with every facility for dealing with all kinds of merchandise, mineral, live stock, and other traffic.

There is a spacious three-storeyed warehouse available for storing cotton, hemp, grain, wool, cement, sugar, and general merchandise.

Ample covered accommodation is afforded for the purpose of handling all kinds of traffic, the stage, as well as the warehouse, being fitted up with the necessary crane power, so that merchandise can be unloaded from carts, lurries, etc., into railway trucks, and vice versa.

Every facility is afforded for dealing with furniture vans, traction engines, carriages, "roundabouts," and other vehicles on wheels.

The crane power available is capable of lifting up to eleven tons, and all kinds of machinery, etc., can be safely handled.

The station is conveniently situated for dealing with traffic to and from the town of Stockport, including Bramhall, Brinksway, Brinnington, Portwood, Davenport, Edgeley, Heaton Norris, Cheadle Heath, Offerton, Heaviley, Adswood, Reddish, Heaton Moor, Heaton Chapel, etc., in connection with shops, warehouses, mills, works, and other places of business.

Ample accommodation is also provided for dealing with horses, cattle, sheep, and other live stock.

Every facility is given for dealing with coke, sand, etc., which can be tipped direct from the carts into railway trucks.

GEORGE'S ROAD, STOCKPORT.—The Cheshire Lines affords every facility at the George's Road Depôt for dealing with coal, coke, stone, iron, and other mineral traffic, as well as timber.

PORTWOOD DEPÔT, STOCKPORT.—The Cheshire Lines Depôt at Portwood is situated at the East end of the town of Stockport, where grain, cotton, sugar, etc., can be dealt with in connection with the various works and mills, etc., in that district. A special warehouse, level with the roadway, has been provided for the storage of cotton.

All traffic should be ordered " Per Cheshire Lines Railway."

Telephone Numbers ... ... **Passenger Dept.—48.**
Goods Dept.—27.

An efficient train service is run to and from Manchester and Chester, suitable for business or residential purposes, and also giving connections with the trunk lines of the London and North Eastern and London, Midland and Scottish Companies.

Northwich Station is provided with accommodation for dealing with all classes of general merchandise, mineral, and passenger train traffic.

There is a commodious warehouse provided for the storage of merchandise, etc.

Provision is made for dealing with horses, carriages, furniture vans, portable engines, and machines on wheels, also live stock and agricultural implements. Crane power with a lifting capacity of five tons is provided.

The Cheshire Lines has direct rail access at Northwich to the following firms and works :—

Brunner, Mond & Co., Ltd.	East Sidings.
Brunner, Mond & Co., Ltd.	Dunkirk Brine Shaft, Marston Branch.
Salt Union Ltd.—	
Adelaide Works	Marston Branch.
Victoria Works	,,
Coronation Shaft	,,
Poole Mine	,,
Old Bank Mine	,,
Ashton's Works	Barons Quay Branch.
Barons Quay Wharf	,,
New Cheshire Salt Co., Ltd.	Marston Branch.
Ingram, Thompson & Sons	,,
Chas. Roberts & Co., Ltd.	,,
J. Richardson & Son	,,
Exors. of S. Appleton	Barons Quay Branch.
Northwich Gas Co.	,,
Moore and Brock, Builders' Merchants.	,,
Northwich Carrying Co., Ltd.	,,
Mersey, Weaver, and Ship Canal Carrying Co., Ltd.	,,
S. Hutton and Co., Public Works Contractors	,,
James Littler and Son, Ltd., Timber Merchants	,,
Geo. Howard Ltd.	,,

HARTFORD AND GREENBANK STATION.

Telephone Number ... ... **95 Northwich.**

The Cheshire Lines Station at Hartford and Greenbank, near Northwich, has facilities for dealing with horses, general merchandise, milk, mineral, and passenger train traffic. A crane is provided with a maximum lifting capacity of five tons.

All traffic should be ordered " Per Cheshire Lines Railway."

Photographs were supplied by the following:

H. C. Casserley — *12, 21, 30, 38, 39, 40, 47, 51, 75, 76, 77, 78*

R. M. Casserley — *9, 33*

J. A. Peden — *3, 6, 7, 19, 49, 53, 65, 66, 68*

J. Hague — *37*

Heyday Publishing Co. — *15, 17, 20, 22, 23, 24, 25, 28, 29, 32, 34, 36, 41, 43, 54, 55, 58*

T. G. Flinders — *69, 70, 71, 72*

A. Johnson — *2, 4, 8, 10, 11*

G. H. Platt — *5*

Author — *1, 13, 14, 16, 18, 26, 27, 31, 35, 42, 44, 45, 46, 48, 50, 57, 61, 62, 63, 64, 67, 73, 74*

Liverpool Loco.
  Preservation Group — *52, 59, 60*

By the same Author:–

'The Cheshire Lines Railway' (as R. P. Griffiths)   Oakwood Press

'The Railways of Manchester'

'The Railways of Leeds & Bradford'

Designed and Printed by Swannack, Brown & Co. Ltd., 13a Anlaby Road, Hull.